Things to Know Before Investing in a Precision Steel Fabricator in England

Table of Contents

Introduction

Investing in a precision steel fabricator in England can be a smart financial decision for any businesses that require high-quality metal components. However, before entering into a business arrangement with a steel fabricator, it is important to have a clear understanding of the terminology used in the industry. This glossary-type book, "Things to Know Before Investing in a Precision Steel Fabricator in England" is designed to provide you with a comprehensive list of terms and definitions commonly used in the precision steel fabrication industry. Whether you are a seasoned investor or just starting out, this book will help you navigate the complex world of precision steel fabrication and make informed decisions when investing in this industry.

Abrasion Resistance

The ability of a steel product to withstand friction caused by wear and tear during operation. Precision steel fabricators must ensure the finished product can withstand any potential abrasion to meet the expected lifespan and functionality requirements.

Accreditation

A standard certification given to a precision steel fabricator after being audited and verified to have met the British and international standards for quality management systems. Certification assures clients of a company's ability to meet customer requirements and provide consistent quality services/products.

Alloy

A combination of different metals resulting in the enhanced mechanical and physical properties of the final product. Precision steel fabricators must choose the right alloy for every project, considering the desired finished product's strength, corrosion resistance, and durability.

Annealing

A heat treatment process done to steel to improve its mechanical properties. Precision steel fabricators use annealing to soften the metal, making it more malleable, easier to work on, and less susceptible to cracking.

Approval

A certificate issued by a client or regulatory body verifying that the finished product is of satisfactory quality and meets all requirements. Precision steel fabricators must aim to deliver finished products that meet customers' approval and pass any regulatory standards.

Architectural steelwork

Steel products that form part of buildings, such as balustrades, handrails, and steel decking. Precision steel fabricators should understand the different regulations and standards governing designing, manufacturing, and installing architectural steelwork to ensure compliance and safety.

Assembly

The act of putting different steel components together to form a complete product. Precision steel fabricators should ensure that every component is correctly assembled to the proper specifications and tolerances.

Assembly tolerances

Precise limits within which components must fit, ensuring that the finished product meets exact design specifications. Precision steel fabricators must work within defined tolerances and ensure that the finished product meets the desired functionality requirements.

Austenitic steel

A type of steel that has a high concentration of nickel and chromium, making it highly corrosion resistant. Precision steel fabricators use austenitic steel where resistance to corrosion and staining is paramount, such as in marine environments.

Automotive steelwork

Products made of steel for use in the automotive industry. Precision steel fabricators should be conversant with industry requirements and standards, ensuring that the products meet the necessary strength, resistance, and durability requirements.

Bar Stock

A type of metal stock that is readily available in standard sizes and shapes, typically round, square, or rectangular in cross-section. Bar stock is a common starting material for precision steel fabrication, and is often used to create shafts, pins, and other components.

Bending

The process of shaping a piece of metal using force to bend it into a desired shape. This can be done by hand or using specialized machinery, and is a common technique used in precision steel fabrication. Before investing in a precision steel fabricator in England, it is important to understand the capabilities of their bending equipment and the types of shapes they can produce.

Bending Radius

The minimum radius that a piece of metal can be bent without causing significant deformation or damage. Before investing in a precision steel fabricator in England, it is important to understand the bending radius limits of their equipment and the types of shapes they can produce.

Bidirectional Tolerance

A term used to describe the acceptable range of deviation from a specified measurement in both positive and negative directions. This is an important term to understand before investing in a precision steel fabricator in England because it describes the degree to which a part or component can vary from the desired specifications. Bidirectional tolerance can help ensure that parts will fit and function properly, and can also affect the cost of production.

Billet

A solid block of steel or other metal, typically rectangular in shape, that is used as a starting material for precision steel fabrication. Understanding the types of billets used by a precision steel fabricator in England can provide insight into their production capabilities and the quality of their work.

Blacksmith

A skilled worker who works with metal, typically heating it in a forge and shaping it through hammering, bending, and other techniques. While blacksmithing is an ancient craft, today's precision steel fabricators in England use modern equipment and techniques to create precise, custom components.

Blueprint

A detailed technical drawing that shows the dimensions, tolerances, and other specifications for a part or component. Before investing in a precision steel fabricator in England, it is important to review their blueprints to ensure that their work meets your requirements and specifications.

Bottleneck

A point in a production process where the velocity or flow of work is limited because of a lack of resources or capacity. This can be a major issue for precision steel fabricators in England, as delays or slowdowns at a single bottleneck can impact the entire production line.

Brazing

A metal-joining process in which two pieces of metal are joined together by heating them to a temperature above 450°C and introducing a filler metal, which flows into the joint and solidifies. This is a common technique used in precision steel fabrication, as it can be used to join dissimilar metals or create complex shapes.

British Standards Institution (BSI)

The national standards body of the United Kingdom, responsible for developing and publishing technical standards across a wide range of industries. Understanding the standards and certifications held by a precision steel fabricator in England can help ensure that their work meets industry requirements and satisfies customer needs.

Capability

The range of skills and equipment that a precision steel fabricator possesses is its capability. Before investing in a precision steel fabricator, it is important to evaluate their capability to ensure they can complete your project to your desired specifications. Factors to consider include the size and complexity of the project as well as the type of material the fabricator can work with.

Capacity

A precision steel fabricator's capacity refers to their ability to handle large or complex projects. Before investing, consider the size and scope of your project and ensure that your chosen fabricator has the capacity to meet your needs. Ask about their experience with similar projects and whether they have the necessary equipment and staff to complete your project in a timely and efficient manner.

Certification

A certification from recognized organizations such as the American Welding Society or the International Organization for Standardization ensures that the precision steel fabricator meets industry standards for quality and safety. Before investing, check if your chosen fabricator has relevant certifications to guarantee the quality of their work.

CNC

Computer numerical control (CNC) is a technology that uses computers to control machine tools such as lathes, mills, routers, and grinders. CNC machines are used in precision steel fabrication to ensure accuracy, speed, and consistent quality. Before investing in a precision steel fabricator, it's important to inquire about their use of CNC technology and their proficiency in operating the machines.

Coating

A protective coating is often applied to steel products to prevent corrosion and wear. The type of coating and application method used by a precision steel fabricator is important when investing. Look for a fabricator who uses high-quality coatings that are appropriate for your project's environment and who applies the coatings with precision and care.

Consistency

Consistency is key in precision steel fabrication. A fabricator who can consistently produce high-quality products with minimal variation is critical when investing. Ask about the fabricator's quality control processes and their commitment to ensuring consistently excellent results.

Cost

The cost of precision steel fabrication can vary widely depending on the complexity of the project, the type of materials used, and the level of customization required. Before investing, ask for detailed quotes from several fabricators to ensure that you get the best value for your investment.

Customer Service

The quality of customer service provided by a precision steel fabricator is an important consideration before investing. A fabricator with excellent customer service can help you navigate the fabrication process, answer your questions, and keep you updated on the progress of your project. Look for a fabricator who is responsive, communicative, and committed to meeting your needs.

Customization

Precision steel fabrication is often used to create unique or custom projects. A precision steel fabricator's ability to customize products to meet their clients' unique needs is an essential consideration when investing. Ask about the fabricator's experience in custom work, the materials they can work with, and their process for creating custom projects.

Cutting

Steel cutting is a critical process in precision steel fabrication. The cutting method used by a fabricator can affect the quality of the final product. Common steel cutting methods include plasma cutting, laser cutting, and water jet cutting. Before investing, inquire about the fabricator's cutting method and the accuracy and precision of their cuts.

Defect Control

Identifying and eliminating welding and fabrication defects should be a top priority for precision steel fabricators in England. Quality control protocols must be in place to catch and fix potential issues before they become problematic. These can include non-destructive testing techniques, such as radiography or ultrasound, to ensure product integrity.

Delivery Times

A critical consideration for investors in precision steel fabrication is how soon the finished product will be delivered. It's important to know the company's turnaround time before investing to determine if it would align with your timeline.

Design Capabilities

Precision steel fabricators in England must have the technological expertise to support the design process for new goods. These capabilities aid in the creation of precise and reliable prototypes and finished products that meet the customer's requirements. This could include the use of computer-aided design software (CAD), which enables a more detailed and accurate 3D model of the product.

Detailed Quotations

Precise, detailed quotations can help investors in determining if the cost of fabrication meets their budget. Detailed quotations should outline the materials, labor, and other fees associated with the fabrication.

Development Process

It is essential that precise steel fabricators in England have multiple stages of product development in place. This aids in the creation of prototypes, identification of any design problems, and adjustment to the product before it enters into mass production. A well-designed development process should encourage communication between the fabricator and the customer.

Dimensional Tolerance

It refers to the amount of variation permitted in the dimensions of a fabricated steel product. High accuracy may necessitate tighter tolerances, which would cost more in manufacturing. It's crucial to recognize the tolerance required for your application to avoid costly over-engineering.

Documentation

All documentation related to the fabrication project, such as certifications or inspection records, should be accessible from the precision steel fabricator. Accurate records can be useful for warranty and legal purposes and are a sign of a reputable and high-quality fabricator.

Documentation Control

All documents related to product fabrication, such as inspection records or material certifications, should be kept under strict control. A lack of control over such records can lead to confusion, unnecessary expense, or legal problems.

Drawing Review

Before beginning the fabrication process, precision steel fabricators in England should thoroughly review any drawing or modeling that the customer has provided. Review ensures that the customer's specifications will be met by the final product.

Durability

Precision steel fabricators must use materials that have a high degree of durability, especially for products that will be used in harsh environments. Corrosion-resistant metals, such as stainless steel or galvanized steel, should be a priority.

Engineering Drawings

Technical documents that contain detailed information about the specifications and requirements of a product, including measurements, materials, and tolerances. Precision steel fabricators rely on engineering drawings to ensure that the final product meets the client's expectations and specifications. These drawings are essential in communicating design and manufacturing instructions between the precision steel fabricator and their client.

Equipment

Precision steel fabricators rely on specialized equipment to produce high-quality products with tight tolerances. These may include CNC machines, laser cutters, press brakes, welding equipment, and saws, among others. Choosing the right equipment is critical to ensuring precision and accuracy in the manufacturing process.

Estimating

A process that involves approximating the cost of a project before it is executed. Precision steel fabricators use estimating to determine the cost of labor, materials, equipment, and other expenses required to complete a project. Accurate estimating is crucial to delivering a product within the client's budget. It involves analyzing the engineering drawings, selecting appropriate manufacturing processes, and calculating time and costs.

Fabrication Process

The process by which raw materials are manipulated into the final product. In steel fabrication, this includes cutting, bending and welding. Understanding the fabrication process is key to knowing the quality of the final product and being able to communicate effectively with the fabricator.

Fasteners

Hardware used to connect two or more parts together. Fasteners can include screws, bolts, nuts, and washers, and are an essential part of steel fabrication. Choosing the right fastener for a given application requires knowledge of the loads and stresses the joints will be subjected to, as well as the materials being used.

Finishing

The process of treating the surface of the steel to protect it from corrosion and to create a desired look or feel. Finishing can include galvanizing, painting, powder coating or sandblasting and can significantly impact the final product's appearance and longevity.

Fire Protection

The use of coatings or other materials to protect steel structures from fire damage. Fire protection is especially important for structures where fire safety is a concern, such as high-rise buildings or industrial sites.

Fit

The precision with which parts fit together. Poor fit can result in weak and unstable structures or products, while good fit can increase strength, decrease weight, and improve durability. Precise fit requires careful measurement, machining, and assembly.

Flange

A projecting flat rim or edge on a steel part designed for connecting or fastening to other parts. Flanges are an important aspect of steel fabrication as they help to hold parts together and distribute loads.

Flatness

The degree to which a surface is flat or level. In precision steel fabrication, flatness is a critical factor in determining the strength, stability, and aesthetics of the final product. Flatness is often measured using specialized equipment such as a surface plate or laser alignment system.

Forming

The process of creating 3D shapes in steel. Forming is often used to create more complex parts where 2D cutting and bending is not enough. Forming requires specialized equipment and expertise in order to achieve the right tolerances and shape.

Fracture Toughness

A measure of how resistant a material is to the propagation of cracks. Steel with high fracture toughness is less prone to failure or cracking under stress, making it more suitable for high-stress applications such as construction or manufacturing.

Fusion Welding

A welding process in which two pieces of steel are joined together by heating them to their melting point and allowing them to fuse together. Fusion welding is often used when a strong, permanent joint is required and is one of the most common types of welding used in steel fabrication.

Galvanized steel

A type of steel that has been coated with a layer of zinc to protect it from corrosion. Before investing in a precision steel fabricator in England, it is important to understand the advantages and disadvantages of using galvanized steel for your project, as well as how it compares to other types of steel.

Galvanizing

The process of coating steel with a layer of zinc to protect it from corrosion. Before investing in a precision steel fabricator in England, it is important to understand if they offer galvanizing services as it can increase the longevity and durability of the steel products. Additionally, inquire about the thickness of the zinc layer, as a thicker layer will provide more protection.

Gas cutting

A process that uses a controlled flame to cut through steel. It is important to understand if a precision steel fabricator offers gas cutting services as it can provide a cost-effective option for cutting thicker sheets of steel.

Gauge

The thickness of a sheet of steel, with a lower gauge meaning a thicker sheet. When investing in a precision steel fabricator, understanding the different gauges that they offer is important in determining if they can provide the specific thickness needed for your project.

Grade

The specific classification of a type of steel based on its physical and chemical properties. Understanding the different grades of steel offered by a precision steel fabricator can ensure that the chosen grade has the desired characteristics for the intended application.

Grain structure

The pattern of metallic crystals within a piece of steel. Understanding the grain structure of the steel being used is important in predicting its behaviour and strength under varying conditions. Before investing in a precision steel fabricator, inquire about their knowledge and understanding of grain structure.

Grinding

The process of smoothing and shaping metal surfaces. Investing in a precision steel fabricator that has grinding capabilities can ensure that your finished product has a polished and smooth appearance.

Grinding angle

The angle at which the grinding wheel is positioned during the grinding process. Understanding the grinding angle used by a precision steel fabricator can ensure that the finished product has the desired shape and finish.

Grooving

The process of creating a groove or channel in a piece of steel. A precision steel fabricator that offers grooving services can create customized shapes and designs in the steel to fit specific project requirements.

Guillotine

A machine used to cut sheet metal with high precision. A precision steel fabricator that has a guillotine can ensure accuracy and consistency in cutting the steel sheets to the desired size and shape.

Hardfacing

A process of applying a hard, wear-resistant alloy to the surface of steel parts to improve their durability and longevity. Hardfacing is commonly used in industries such as mining, construction, and manufacturing to extend the lifespan of critical equipment and machinery.

Hardness Testing

A process of measuring the hardness of a material, often used in precision steel fabrication to ensure that the steel is of the required quality and durability. This is done using specialized equipment that measures the resistance of the steel to indentation or scratching.

Heat Treatment

A process used in precision steel fabrication that involves heating and cooling steel to strengthen or alter its properties for specific applications. Heat treatment also helps to prevent corrosion and reduce wear and tear on the steel.

High-Strength Low-Alloy Steel

A type of steel that contains small amounts of alloying elements such as manganese, molybdenum, and chromium. This type of steel is used in precision steel fabrication to produce parts that are both strong and lightweight.

Hollow Structural Sections

A type of steel tube used in precision steel fabrication that has a hollow interior and a square, rectangular, or circular cross-section. These sections are often used in construction for their strength, durability, and ability to withstand heavy loads.

Hot Rolled Steel

A method of producing steel that involves heating billets or ingots to a high temperature and then rolling them into thin sheets or plates. Hot rolled steel is known for its strength and durability, making it a popular choice in precision steel fabrication for applications such as construction and industrial equipment.

Hot Work Tool Steel

A type of steel that is specifically designed for use in high-temperature environments, such as those encountered in precision steel fabrication processes. Hot work tool steel is known for its strength, toughness, and resistance to thermal shock, making it an ideal choice for tools and dies used in metalworking processes.

Hot-Dip Galvanizing

A process of coating steel with a protective layer of zinc by immersing it in a bath of molten zinc. Hot-dip galvanizing is used to protect steel from corrosion and rust, which can weaken its structural integrity.

Hydraulic Shearing

A cutting method used in precision steel fabrication that uses hydraulic power to cut and shape steel plates. This method is commonly used for cutting thick and large steel plates.

Hydroforming

A process of shaping metal tubes or sheets by using a fluid to apply pressure from the inside out. Hydroforming is used in precision steel fabrication to create complex shapes and designs that are difficult to achieve using traditional methods.

Jet Cutting

A high-precision cutting method that utilizes a high-pressure jet of water mixed with abrasive materials to cut through thick steel. This technique is commonly used in precision steel fabrication in England, especially for complex designs that require cutting intricate patterns.

Jhook

A term used for the shape of the end of a steel rod or bar that has a 90-degree bend, allowing it to be easily secured to another piece of metal through welding or bolting.

JIC Fittings

A type of hydraulic fittings used to connect fluid carrying pipes or hoses, commonly used in the precision steel fabricator industry in England, especially in hydraulic systems.

Jig

A tool used to guide and shape raw materials, such as metal sheets or tubes, during the manufacturing process for precision steel fabrication. Jigs are often custom-made for a specific project to ensure accuracy in shape and size.

Jig Bore

A high-precision machining tool used to create holes in metal pieces, often for the creation of complex assemblies in precision steel fabrication in England.

Job Shop

A company that specializes in producing custom-made parts or products to order. Precision steel fabricators in England often operate as job shops, providing high-quality products tailored to individual customer specifications.

Joggle

A term used for the process of forming an offset in a piece of metal, creating a lap joint that increases the strength of the connection.

Joining Techniques

The term used for various methods used to join metal pieces together, be it by welding, riveting, or screwing. These techniques are vital in the precision steel fabricator trade in England, as they ensure the final product is structurally sound.

Jominy End Quench Test

A test used to measure the hardenability of a steel alloy, essential in the precision steel fabricator trade, ensuring the final product meets the desired mechanical properties for its intended use.

Just-In-Time (JIT)

A manufacturing philosophy that minimizes inventory and production times, reducing waste and overhead costs. Precision steel fabricators in England often use this approach to remain competitive in the industry.

Kaizen

A Japanese word meaning "continuous improvement." Kaizen is an approach to Lean manufacturing that emphasizes making small, incremental improvements to processes and procedures over time. In a precision steel fabrication context, Kaizen may involve identifying and eliminating waste, reducing production time, or improving workplace safety. Adopting a Kaizen approach can help to foster a culture of continuous improvement and innovation.

Kanban

A Lean manufacturing tool used to visualize and manage the production process. Kanban involves using cards, typically color-coded, to signal the need for additional inputs or the completion of particular tasks. In a precision steel fabrication context, Kanban may be used to manage the flow of raw materials, track work in progress, and ensure timely completion of orders. The adoption of Kanban can help to increase efficiency, reduce errors, and improve production planning.

Key Account Management

A customer-focused sales strategy that aims to build long-term, profitable relationships with key customers. In a precision steel fabrication context, key account management may involve identifying target customers, developing customized solutions, and providing value-added services. Effective key account management can help to increase revenue, build brand loyalty, and reduce customer churn.

Key Performance Indicators (KPI)

Measurable values used to determine the success and progress of a precision steel fabricator's operations, such as accuracy of cuts, efficiency of production, and customer satisfaction. KPIs provide essential data for decision-making and identifying areas for improvement. The use of KPIs can be crucial for investors to evaluate the company's overall performance and future potential.

Key Performance Questions (KPQs)

A set of questions used to focus analysis and identify critical success factors. In the context of investing in a precision steel fabricator, KPQs may include questions about the company's financial performance, customer retention rates, or technological capabilities. Using KPQs can help investors to evaluate the potential risks and rewards of investing in a particular company.

Kitting

The process of assembling components into a kit or bundle for use in manufacturing or other applications. In a precision steel fabrication context, kitting may involve assembling parts into kits for specific orders or projects, or creating pre-assembled components for use in larger products. Kitting can help to streamline the production process, reduce waste, and increase efficiency.

Knowledge Base

A centralized repository of information and knowledge used to support decision-making and problem-solving within a company. In a precision steel fabrication context, a knowledge base may include information on raw materials, production processes, quality control measures, customer requirements, and regulatory compliance issues. Maintaining a comprehensive knowledge base can help to ensure that critical information is accessible to employees when it is needed, reducing the risks of errors and delays.

Knowledge Management

A systematic approach to managing and creating knowledge within a company, including processes, tools, and techniques. In the context of a precision steel fabricator, knowledge management aims to capture, organize, and share information related to the use of new technology, efficient production methods, the sourcing of raw materials, and relevant regulatory requirements, among other things. Knowledge management can be a critical tool for ensuring the continuity of operations and minimizing the risks of turnover among key employees.

Knowledge Transfer

The process of sharing knowledge and expertise between people or departments within a company. Knowledge transfer is important for ensuring that critical knowledge is not lost when employees leave or retire, and that best practices are shared throughout the organization. In a precision steel fabrication context, knowledge transfer may involve documenting production processes, training new employees, or creating standard operating procedures.

Laser Cutting

The use of a laser beam to cut through steel with precision and accuracy. It creates clean, precise edges which reduce the need for further finishing or processing. Laser cutting is often used for intricate designs, and is a common method used by precision steel fabricators in England.

Laser Welding

A method of welding that uses laser beams to generate high amounts of heat to melt and join two pieces of metal together. Laser welding is a precise, low-heat method that produces clean, strong welds that require minimal finishing.

Lead Time

The time it takes for a precision steel fabricator to complete a project from initial design to delivery. It is crucial to determine the lead time required to complete a project, in order to meet the customer's expectations and plan accordingly.

Level of Expertise

A measure of a precision steel fabricator's knowledge, skill and experience in their respective field. Before investing, it is important to check the level of expertise of the fabricator to avoid costly mistakes and ensure that the project deadlines are met on time.

Liability Insurance

A type of insurance that protects a precision steel fabricator from claims arising from damage or injury resulting from their work. A reliable fabricator should have liability insurance in place in order to protect themselves and their clients against potential financial losses or injuries.

Lifting Capacity

A measure of the maximum weight that can be lifted by a crane, hoist or other lifting device. Lifting capacity is an important consideration when planning and executing heavy steel fabrication projects.

Load-Bearing Capacity

The maximum amount of weight that a structure can support without collapsing or failing. Load-bearing capacity is an important consideration when designing and building steel structures, in order to ensure structural integrity and safety.

Logistic Planning

The process of planning and coordinating the movement and delivery of materials, equipment and finished products. Good logistic planning is essential for the success of a project as it ensures that the required resources are available at the right place and time.

Long-Term Relationship

The development of a lasting partnership between a precision steel fabricator and a customer. This relationship is built on trust, mutual respect and shared goals, and is essential for the success of future projects. Long-term relationships can result in better communication, increased efficiency and overall success.

Machining

Machining is the process of using various tools to remove material from the surface of a workpiece to achieve the desired shape and size. It involves cutting, drilling, milling, and turning. A precision steel fabricator should have a dedicated machining department to ensure accuracy and quality in the production process.

Manufacturing Process

The manufacturing process is the series of steps involved in converting raw materials into a finished product. In precision steel fabrication, the process includes material selection, cutting, forming, welding, finishing, and assembly. A well-defined and controlled manufacturing process is critical to delivering quality products consistently.

Material Characteristics

Material characteristics refer to the properties of a particular metal that determine its suitability for specific applications. Factors like hardness, strength, and ductility play a crucial role in the selection of material for precision steel fabrication. The material's properties influence the forming process, the level of precision achievable, and the final product's performance.

Material Selection

Choosing the right material is crucial in precision steel fabrication as it influences the product's strength, durability, and cost. Common materials used include stainless steel, aluminum, and carbon steel. The selection process considers factors like environmental conditions, load, and weight-bearing capacity.

Metal Bending

Metal bending is the process of forming a workpiece into a prescribed shape by applying force to it. It is commonly used in precision steel fabrication to create complex shapes and curves. The process requires a high level of accuracy, and specialized equipment like hydraulic press brakes or rollers is used to achieve it.

Metal Fabrication

Metal fabrication is a broad term that encompasses the entire process of creating metal products from raw materials. It includes cutting, forming, welding, finishing, and assembling various metal components into a usable product. In precision steel fabrication, metal fabrication is done with accuracy and attention to detail.

Metal Finishing

Metal finishing is the process of altering a metal surface's properties to achieve a desired appearance, texture, or functionality. It includes various techniques like polishing, painting, electroplating, anodizing, and powder coating. In precision steel fabrication, metal finishing is done to improve corrosion resistance, durability, and appearance.

Metal Shearing

Metal shearing is the process of cutting sheets or plates of metal into the desired shape using a set of blades. It is a precision process that requires expertise and specialized equipment. Metal shearing is commonly used in precision steel fabrication to create parts with straight edges and accurate dimensions.

Milling

Milling is a machining process that involves the use of rotary cutters to remove material from a workpiece. It is commonly used in precision steel fabrication to create complex shapes or achieve high accuracy, tight tolerances, and a superior surface finish.

Motorized Cutting

Motorized cutting is a process that uses machines to cut metal sheets and plates. It is used primarily to produce precision cuts with minimal waste. Laser cutting, plasma cutting, and water jet cutting are common motorized cutting techniques used in metal fabrication.

National Standards

The precision steel fabricator must meet the UK's national standards for quality control, health and safety, environmental protection, and regulatory compliance. The requirements may vary depending on the industry, product, or application. The fabricator's compliance with the national standards ensures that the products are safe, reliable, and of high quality.

NDA Breach

Any unauthorized disclosure or use of the confidential information protected under the NDA constitutes a breach. The precision steel fabricator is liable for damages, legal action, and reputational loss if it breaches the NDA.

New Product Development

The process of designing, testing, and launching a new precision steel product meets the client's requirements and industry standards. It involves market research, concept development, prototyping, testing, and branding. The precision steel fabricator must have the necessary resources, equipment, and expertise to support new product development.

Niche Market

A specialized or narrow segment of the market that requires a unique set of skills, expertise, and capabilities. The precision steel fabricator may focus on a niche market such as defense, aerospace, automotive, or medical equipment. It enables the fabricator to differentiate itself from competitors and offer value-added services to its clients.

Non-Conformance

Any deviation from the agreed specifications, requirements, or tolerances is referred to as non-conformance. It may arise from defects, errors, equipment malfunction, or process failures. The precision steel fabricator must report any non-conformance to the client and take corrective actions to prevent reoccurrence.

Non-Destructive Testing (NDT)

A set of techniques used to inspect, measure, and evaluate the properties of materials and components without causing damage or altering their integrity. The precision steel fabricator may use NDT methods such as ultrasonic testing, magnetic particle inspection, radiography, or eddy current testing to ensure quality control and detect any defects.

Non-Disclosure Agreements (NDA)

A legal agreement between the precision steel fabricator and the client to maintain confidentiality about any sensitive information shared. It protects the fabricator's trade secrets, intellectual property rights, and prevents any sharing of sensitive information with third parties.

Non-Refundable Deposits

The precision steel fabricator may require a non-refundable deposit from the client to cover initial design, prototyping, and production costs. The deposit ensures that the client is committed to the project, and the fabricator has sufficient funds to start the work. The exact amount and terms of the deposit are negotiable between the parties.

Non-Tariff Barriers

Any trade restrictions, regulations, or policies imposed by the government or the industry that affect the precision steel fabricator's international trade. Examples include import quotas, technical standards, sanitary and phytosanitary measures, and licensing requirements. The non-tariff barriers may limit the fabricator's access to new markets, increase costs, or create unfair competition. Therefore, the fabricator must be aware of the relevant regulations and seek professional advice to mitigate the risks.

Nurturing Customer Relationships

Building and maintaining long-term partnerships with clients by understanding their needs, delivering quality products, providing excellent customer service, and offering after-sales support. The precision steel fabricator needs to establish a good reputation, promote transparency, and communicate effectively with the clients to enhance their trust and loyalty.

OEM (Original Equipment Manufacturer)

This refers to a company that produces parts or equipment that are used in another company's product. Precision steel fabricators in England may work with OEM customers to produce custom parts or equipment that meet specific requirements. It is important to understand the OEM customer's requirements and specifications to ensure that the production meets their needs.

Offshore manufacturing

This is the process of producing goods in a foreign country, often for cost savings. Precision steel fabricators in England may choose to offshore certain manufacturing tasks to countries like China, India, or Mexico to take advantage of lower labor costs. However, offshore manufacturing can also lead to quality control issues, communication problems, and delays. It is important to carefully consider the advantages and disadvantages of offshore manufacturing before making a decision.

Online reviews

These are customer reviews and ratings available online that can provide insight into the quality of work and customer service of a precision steel fabricator in England. It is important to carefully review online reviews and ratings to help determine the reputation and reliability of a precision steel fabricator before investing.

On-time delivery

This refers to the ability of a precision steel fabricator in England to deliver an order on or before the agreed-upon delivery date. Timely delivery is essential in ensuring customer satisfaction and long-term business relationships. It is therefore important to establish clear and realistic delivery expectations, designate a point of contact, and monitor the progress of the order.

Operations Management

This is the process of controlling and overseeing the day-to-day operations of a business to ensure efficiency and productivity. Precision steel fabricators in England rely on strong operations management to ensure that resources are used effectively, production is maximized, and quality is maintained. It is important to understand how a precision steel fabricator manages its operations to ensure optimal performance and quality.

Optimal inventory management

This is the process of managing inventory levels to ensure that they are neither too high nor too low. Precision steel fabricators in England rely on optimal inventory management to ensure that they have the necessary raw materials on hand to complete orders without incurring unnecessary costs associated with overstocking or stockouts. It is important to understand how a precision steel fabricator manages its inventory to ensure timely delivery and cost savings.

Order lead time

This is the time required to process an order from the time it is placed until it is delivered. Precision steel fabricators in England typically have a lead time that can vary depending on the complexity of the order, the availability of materials, and the workload. It is crucial to ask about the order lead time before placing an order to avoid delays and ensure timely delivery.

Outsourcing

This refers to the process of hiring a third-party company to perform specific tasks instead of performing them in-house. Many precision steel fabricators in England outsource certain tasks such as painting or coating for cost and efficiency reasons. It is important to know which tasks are being outsourced and to whom, to ensure quality control and timely delivery.

Outsourcing limitations

This refers to the potential drawbacks of outsourcing certain tasks to third-party companies. While outsourcing can offer cost savings and efficiency benefits, it can also lead to quality control issues, communication problems, and delays. Understanding the limitations of outsourcing is crucial in determining which tasks should be performed in-house and which should be outsourced.

Overhead costs

This refers to the expenses a precision steel fabricator in England incurs in the course of doing business that are not related to specific tasks or projects. Examples of overhead costs include rent, utilities, salaries, and insurance. It is important to understand the overhead costs associated with a precision steel fabricator to determine the true cost of their services.

Packaging and transportation

Packaging and transportation refer to the process of packing finished steel products for shipping and delivering them to customers. It is important to choose a precision steel fabricator who has experience in packaging and transportation to ensure products are delivered safely and on time.

Payment terms

Payment terms refer to the conditions under which a precision steel fabricator expects to be paid for their products or services. Before investing in a fabricator, it is important to understand their payment terms to avoid any payment disputes or confusion.

Precision cutting

Precision cutting is a method of cutting steel products accurately and consistently using advanced cutting machinery such as laser, plasma, and waterjet cutters. Precision cutting can result in high-quality and precise finished products.

Precision steel fabricator

A precision steel fabricator is a company that specializes in the manufacturing of high-quality steel products using advanced machinery and techniques. They can provide a wide range of steel fabrication services, such as welding, cutting, bending, and finishing to meet the custom needs of their clients.

Price competitiveness

Price competitiveness refers to the ability of a precision steel fabricator to offer quality products at a competitive price. When investing in a fabricator, it is important to compare their prices with other fabricators to ensure that their prices are reasonable and competitive.

Production capacity

Production capacity refers to the maximum amount of products that a precision steel fabricator can produce within a given time frame. It is important to know the production capacity of a fabricator before investing in them to ensure that they can meet your required output level.

Production quality control

Production quality control is a process of ensuring that fabricated steel products meet the specified quality standards. It involves checking raw materials, manufacturing processes, manufacturing equipment, and finished products for defects or errors.

Professionalism

Professionalism refers to the conduct, behavior, and attitude of a precision steel fabricator towards their clients. Good professionalism is key when investing in a fabricator as it can build a good relationship, leading to good communication, better services, and overall satisfaction.

Project management

Project management refers to the process of planning, organizing, and directing resources to achieve specific project goals. When choosing a precision steel fabricator, it is important to consider their project management capabilities to ensure that they can deliver quality products within the specified timeline and budget.

Prototyping

Prototyping is the process of creating a sample or model of a product before starting large-scale production. Investing in a precision steel fabricator who can offer prototyping services can be beneficial in the development of custom-designed steel products.

Quality Assurance

Quality assurance is the process of ensuring that the precision steel fabrication process is done to the required standards and specifications. A good precision steel fabricator in England should have a comprehensive quality assurance process that involves regular inspections, testing, and analysis of the products.

Quality Control

Quality control is an essential aspect of precision steel fabrication that refers to the process of ensuring the final product meets the required specifications and standards. A good precision steel fabricator in England should have a comprehensive quality control process that identifies potential issues and rectifies them before the final product is delivered to the client.

Quality Control Inspector

A quality control inspector is a professional responsible for ensuring that the final product meets the required standards and specifications. A good precision steel fabricator in England should have a team of skilled and experienced quality control inspectors who can identify potential issues and rectify them before the final product is delivered to the client.

Quality Management

Quality management refers to the process of ensuring that the precision steel fabrication process meets the required standards and specifications. A good precision steel fabricator in England should have a comprehensive quality management process that involves regular inspections, testing, and analysis of the products.

Quality Standards

Quality standards refer to the set of rules and regulations that a precision steel fabricator must adhere to to ensure that the final product meets the required standards and specifications. A good precision steel fabricator in England should be aware of and follow all the relevant quality standards and regulations.

Quantitative Analysis

Quantitative analysis in precision steel fabrication involves the use of mathematical and statistical methods to measure and analyze data. A good precision steel fabricator should be able to use quantitative analysis to accurately determine the strength, durability, and other properties of the steel fabrication products.

Quenching

Quenching is a heat treatment process used in precision steel fabrication to harden the steel. It involves heating the steel to a high temperature and then rapidly cooling it in water or oil, which results in a more durable and stronger material.

Quick Turnaround

Quick turnaround refers to the ability of a precision steel fabricator to quickly produce and deliver high-quality steel fabrication products to its clients. A good precision steel fabricator in England should have the resources and expertise to deliver products within a short period without compromising on quality.

Quota

A quota is a limit on the amount of steel fabrication products that a precision steel fabricator can produce within a given period. A good precision steel fabricator in England should have the capacity to meet the quotas set by its clients without compromising on quality or timelines.

Quotation

A quotation is an estimate of the cost of a precision steel fabrication project. A precision steel fabricator should provide a detailed quotation that includes all the costs associated with the project, including labor, materials, and overhead costs.

Raw Materials

The basic materials used in the fabrication process of precision steel, such as iron ore, coal, and limestone. Knowing the source and quality of the raw materials can impact the overall quality and cost of the final product.

Regulations

The laws and guidelines put in place by the government to ensure safety, quality, and environmental standards are met in the precision steel fabrication process. It is important to understand and comply with these regulations to avoid penalties and legal action.

Resale Value

The potential value of the fabricated steel product in the secondary market. Understanding the potential resale value can impact the decision-making process when investing in a precision steel fabricator.

Research and Development

The process of researching and developing new methods, equipment, and materials for precision steel fabrication. Keeping up-to-date with new technologies and materials can improve the efficiency and quality of the fabrication process.

Resources

The various tools, equipment, and personnel necessary for the fabrication process, including skilled workers, engineering software, and welding machines. Ensuring adequate resources are available can impact the quality and speed of the fabrication process.

Risk Management

The process of identifying and mitigating potential risks and hazards associated with precision steel fabrication, such as safety risks, supply chain disruptions, and quality control issues. Effective risk management can minimize the impact of these risks on the final product.

Robotic Automation

The use of robots and automated machinery in the precision steel fabrication process. Understanding the capabilities and limitations of these machines can impact the speed and quality of the fabrication process.

Roll Forming

A specialized process used for shaping and bending steel into complex shapes and profiles. Knowing if the precision steel fabricator has the necessary roll forming capabilities can impact the overall quality and cost of the final product.

Root Cause Analysis

A problem-solving technique used to identify the underlying causes of quality issues or defects in the steel fabrication process. Conducting root cause analysis can help pinpoint areas for improvement in the precision steel fabrication process.

Rust Prevention

The application of coatings or treatments to prevent corrosion and rusting of the steel product. Understanding the types of rust prevention methods used by the precision steel fabricator can impact the durability and longevity of the final product.

Shop Drawings

Detailed drawings produced by the fabricator that show the dimensions, materials, connections and other features of the steel components to be made and assembled.

Shot Blasting

A surface preparation method that involves projecting tiny metal balls at high speed onto the surface of steel to remove rust, scale and other contaminants.

Steel Alloys

A mixture of two or more different types of metals, where steel is the main component, used to enhance the strength, toughness and durability of steel.

Steel Fabrication

The process of transforming steel into finished products through cutting, bending, welding and assembling.

Steel Fabrication Equipment

The machinery and tools used by steel fabricators to cut, bend, weld and assemble steel, such as saws, shears, drills, plasma cutters and welding machines.

Steel Fabricator Certification

A certification awarded to steel fabricators that demonstrate compliance with industry standards and best practices, such as ISO 9001, CE Marking or BSI Kitemark.

Steel Finish

The final surface treatment applied to steel, such as painting, galvanizing or powder coating, to protect it from corrosion and improve its appearance.

Steel Quality Standards

The set of standards and specifications that define the quality, strength and durability of steel used in different applications, such as ASTM, EN or BS.

Structural Steel

A type of steel specifically designed to be used in construction as structural elements.

Surface Preparation

The process of preparing the surface of steel by cleaning, blasting, sanding or grinding to remove any impurities or contaminants that may affect the quality of the final product.

Technical Drawing

Technical drawing is the process of creating detailed drawings that communicate the client's design requirements. The drawings assist the fabricator in understanding the client's vision to create a quality product. Before investing in a precision steel fabricator, understanding the fabricator's ability to create and interpret technical drawings is paramount in achieving the desired end-product.

Testing

Quality assurance is paramount in precision steel fabrication. Testing ensures that the end-product meets the client's specifications and adheres to the industry's quality standards. Before investing in a precision steel fabricator, understanding the testing procedures the fabricator uses guarantees a quality product and saves you the client both time and money in the long run.

Testing Standards

Testing standards refer to the set guidelines or procedures used to test the quality of the fabricated product. Precision steel fabrication requires adherence to specific testing standards to ensure the product meets the required quality standards. Before investing in a precision steel fabricator, understanding the testing standards the fabricator adheres to is vital to achieving a quality end-product.

Thermal Cutting

Thermal cutting is the process of using a heat source to cut steel sheets or plates to specific shapes and sizes. Precision steel fabrication requires the use of thermal cutting to achieve specific shapes and sizes while maintaining quality. Before investing in a precision steel fabricator, understanding the fabricator's thermal cutting equipment and processes is important in achieving a quality end-product.

TIG Welding

TIG welding, also known as Tungsten Inert Gas Welding, is a welding process that uses a Tungsten Electrode to create precise welds. Precision steel fabrication requires specialized welding equipment and techniques like TIG welding. Before investing in a precision steel fabricator, understanding the fabricator's experience with TIG welding and its importance in achieving a quality product is crucial.

Tolerance

Tolerance refers to the allowable deviation in the dimension or size of the fabricated product. In precision steel fabrication, the tolerance level is very low, and it determines the quality of the finished product. It also dictates the operation and functionality of the equipment for which the steel fabrication is being used. Before investing in a precision steel fabricator, it's crucial to understand the tolerance level the fabricator can achieve and whether it meets your project's requirements.

Tool steel fabrication

Tool steel fabrication involves the production of complex steel tools or dies for use in industrial production. Therefore, a precision steel fabricator must have experience in tool steel fabrication to maintain product quality. Before investing in a precision steel fabricator, understanding the fabricator's experience with tool steel fabrication is critical to producing quality steel products.

Tooling

Tooling is the process of creating molds or dies for the production of steel products. Precision steel fabrication requires the use of specialized tooling equipment to ensure that the final product meets the client's specifications. Before investing in a precision steel fabricator, understanding the type of tooling equipment the fabricator uses and the level of maintenance the equipment gets is critical in achieving a quality product.

Traceability

Traceability is the process of tracking the steel used in fabrication back to its source. Precision steel fabrication requires the use of specific grade steel, which must meet the required specifications. To ensure product quality, the fabricator must establish the steel's identity and traceability back to the manufacturer. Before investing in a precision steel fabricator, understanding the fabricator's traceability procedures ensures that the steel used meets your project's quality standards.

Tube Bending

Tube bending is the process of reshaping steel tubing to achieve specific angles or curves. Precision steel fabrication requires the use of tube bending to achieve specific shapes and sizes while maintaining quality. Before investing in a precision steel fabricator, understanding the fabricator's tube bending equipment and processes is important in achieving a quality end-product.

Ulterior Factors

There are external factors to consider when investing in a precision steel fabricator. These include the fabricator's location, reputation, and the nature of the product required. Investors should examine all these factors before deciding on a fabricator to help them make informed decisions about investment.

Ultra-Precise Tolerances

Precision steel fabricators should be able to maintain ultra-precise tolerances in their production process to provide parts that meet exact specifications. Investors should check that the fabricator has the technical expertise and equipment to maintain these tolerances.

Understand Costs

Investors should understand the costs associated with precision steel fabrication, including material costs, production costs, and any additional costs related to customization, quality control, or delivery.

Understanding Industry Regulations

Precision steel fabrication is regulated by industry standards such as ISO 9001/14001 and European Union CE. Investors should ensure the fabricator adheres to these standards.

Understanding the Production Process

The production process of a precision steel fabricator involves a series of steps such as designing, cutting, welding, finishing, and quality control. An investor needs to understand each step to ensure the final product meets the required specifications and quality standards.

Unique Requirements

An investor should communicate their unique requirements to the fabricator to ensure their product meets their specific needs. Investors should check if the fabricator has the experience and flexibility to work on customized designs.

Unique Selling Proposition

Investors should check if the fabricator has a unique selling proposition, such as competitive pricing, customization, or faster turnaround times, that stands out from its competitors. This aspect can be a differentiator in real-world investment applications.

Usage of Advanced Technologies

Precision steel fabricators use state-of-the-art technologies such as computer-aided design (CAD), computer-aided manufacturing (CAM), and robotics to optimize the production process, ensure accuracy, and reduce production costs. Investors need to ensure the fabricator they choose has up-to-date technology and expertise in deploying it.

Use of Quality Steel

Precision steel fabricators should use high-quality steel to produce parts that meet the required criteria for strength, durability, and resistance. Investors should verify the materials used by the fabricator.

Utilization of Quality Control

Investors should confirm that the fabricator uses documented quality control systems, including inspection procedures and test equipment, to verify that each part meets the required specifications, tolerances, and finish.

Vacuum Heat Treatment

A heat treatment process used to enhance the strength and durability of steel products. Vacuum heat treatment involves heating the steel in a vacuum environment to prevent oxidation and contamination, resulting in a product with improved mechanical properties.

Validation

The process of ensuring that a product meets the required standards and specifications. Validation can help precision steel fabricators in England ensure that their products are of high quality and meet customer expectations.

Value Engineering

A practice that aims to optimize the value of a product by analyzing its functions and costs to determine if any changes can be made to decrease cost without sacrificing quality. This approach can be utilized by precision steel fabricators in England to reduce production costs and increase productivity while still delivering a high-quality product to their customers.

Value Stream Mapping

A technique used by precision steel fabricators in England to analyze and optimize their production process. This involves creating a visual map of the production process, identifying areas of waste and inefficiency, and developing a plan to eliminate them.

Variable Cost

Costs that vary with changes in the level of production output. Variable costs for precision steel fabricators in England may include the cost of raw materials, production labor, and shipping.

Vendor

A person, company, or organization that supplies materials or services to a precision steel fabricator in England. Choosing the right vendor is critical as it can impact the overall quality of the final product.

Vendor Managed Inventory

A system in which a vendor manages the inventory of a precision steel fabricator in England. This approach can help reduce inventory costs and improve the accuracy of inventory forecasting and management.

Vertical Integration

A business strategy used by some precision steel fabricators in England to increase efficiency and control over their supply chain. It involves acquiring other businesses in the supply chain, including suppliers and distributors, to ensure that the company has full control over the entire process.

Vickers Hardness Test

A test used to determine the hardness of materials, including steel. The Vickers hardness test involves indenting the surface of the material with a diamond-shaped indenter and measuring the size of the indentation. This test can help precision steel fabricators in England ensure that their products meet the required specifications for hardness and durability.

Volume Production

A manufacturing technique in which a large number of identical products are produced using standardized processes. This approach is often used by precision steel fabricators in England to increase efficiency and decrease costs.

Waterjet Cutting

Waterjet cutting is a process used by precision steel fabricators that involves using a high-pressure jet of water to cut through metal. This technique allows for precise cuts and is often used when working with sensitive metals.

Weld Inspection

Weld inspection is the process of ensuring that the welding performed by the precision steel fabricator meets specific standards in terms of quality and safety. This includes checking for defects such as porosity, cracking, and distortion that can weaken the welds. It is essential to know the level of weld inspection the fabricator conducts.

Welding

Welding refers to the process of joining two or more pieces of metal by heating them to a certain temperature and applying pressure. A precision steel fabricator in England will likely use welding extensively to create complex structures and ensure their stability. It is important to know the different types of welding they specialize in and whether they have experienced welders on staff.

Welding Codes

Welding codes refer to a set of standards and guidelines that dictate how welding is performed in specific industries. It is important to know whether the precision steel fabricator follows relevant welding codes to ensure the highest quality of work.

Wire EDM

Wire EDM (Electrical Discharge Machining) is a machining process that uses an electrically charged wire to cut through metal with extreme precision. This is a common process used by precision steel fabricators to create intricate shapes and designs.

Work Tolerance

Work tolerance refers to the precision and accuracy that a precision steel fabricator can achieve in their work. A high level of work tolerance is essential when fabricating intricate or complex parts that require precise measurements and tight tolerances. It is important to understand their level of work tolerance when choosing a precision steel fabricator.

Workforce

The workforce of a precision steel fabricator refers to the number and quality of employees responsible for fabricating steel parts. A skilled workforce is key to producing quality steel parts efficiently and quickly.

Workshop Capacity

The workshop capacity refers to the maximum amount of work a precision steel fabricator can handle at one time. Understanding the fabricator's workshop capacity is crucial in determining whether they can fulfill orders within a given timeframe.

Workstation Setup

A workstation setup refers to the way a precision steel fabricator positions and arranges their machines, tools, and equipment to optimize workflow and efficiency. Understanding their workstation setup will provide insight into their level of organization and attention to detail.

WPS (Welding Procedure Specification)

A WPS is a written document that specifies the welding procedure to be used for each particular application. It outlines parameters such as the type of welding process, materials, and settings. Knowing whether the precision steel fabricator has a WPS for each job is crucial in ensuring quality control.